LOVE IS...

Created, published, and distributed by Knock Knock
1635 Electric Ave.
Venice, CA 90291
knockknockstuff.com
Knock Knock is a registered trademark of Knock Knock LLC

Design by Carol Kono-Noble
Illustrations by Harriet Russell

ISBN: 978-1683490084-5
UPC: 825703-50216-9

10 9 8 7 6 5 4 3 2 1

LOVE IS...

A ROLLER COASTER

(and other such sayings)

KNOCK KNOCK.
VENICE, CALIFORNIA

DESCRIBING THE INTANGIBLE

It's pretty obvious that the biggest philosophical questions are notoriously hard to answer. That's why humans turn to comparisons to explain the mysteries of the universe. It's easier to describe one mysterious and incomprehensible thing by noting its similarities to other, more familiar and concrete things.

Ask someone to finish the phrase "Love is..." and you might hear a proverb, a quotation, a saying, or a song lyric. Often, you'll hear a metaphor of some kind. There are as many ways to describe what "love is" as there are grains of sand on a beach (another metaphor—we just can't help ourselves).

But they don't all have the same perspective. Great minds may think alike, but you'll see as you page through this book that there are as many points of view about the subject of "love" as there are stars in the sky (see how easy that is?). Watch how the examples, both cynical and sweet, within this little book complement—and contradict—each other.

LOVE IS LIKE A ROCK.

LOVE IS REAL.

LOVE IS AN ILLUSION.

Love is much nicer
to be in than an
automobile accident,
a tight girdle, a higher
tax bracket, or a
holding pattern
over Philadelphia.

LOVE IS A DAMN NUISANCE.

LOVE IS A BATTLEFIELD.

LOVE IS LIKE A RED, RED ROSE.

LOVE IS PAIN.

LOVE IS MYSTIFYING.

**Love is
a cocktail
of brain
chemicals.**

**Love is not the dying moan
of a distant violin—**

it's the twang of a bedspring.

LOVE IS A ROLLER COASTER.

LOVE IS OLD,
LOVE IS NEW/
LOVE IS ALL,
LOVE IS **YOU**.

Love is magical.

Love is hard.

LOVE IS GRAND.

Love is like an ocean: you can see its beginning but never its end.

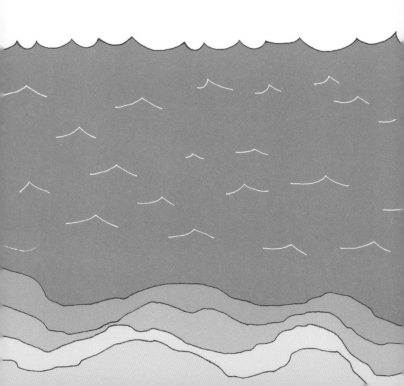

**LOVE IS AN
OPEN DOOR.**

Love is a window.

LOVE IS
BEING
FOUND.

LOVE IS

A GIFT.

LOVE IS
SINGING
KARAOKE
"UNDER
PRESSURE"
AND LETTING
THE OTHER
PERSON SING
THE FREDDIE
MERCURY PART.

Love is loud.

Love is the delightful interval between meeting a beautiful girl and discovering she looks like a haddock.

LOVE IS ENOUGH.

LOVE IS NOT ENOUGH.

Love is in the air.

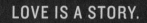
LOVE IS A STORY.

LOVE IS A LIE.

LOVE IS
SIMPLE.

Love is like oxygen / You get too much you get too high / Not enough and you're gonna die.

Love is everything.

Love is nothing.

LOVE IS A RAZOR.

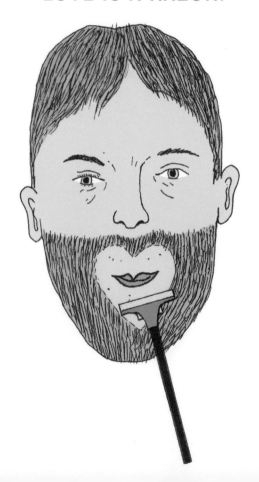

Love is murder.

LOVE IS A RIVER.

LOVE IS A BURNING THING.

LOVE IS THE NEW BLACK.

LOVE IS POWER.

LOVE IS METAPHYSICAL GRAVITY.

Love is strange.

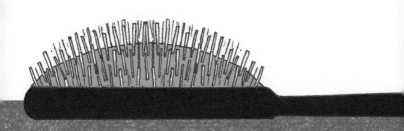

Love is the drug I'm thinking of.

LOVE IS STRONGER THAN DEATH.

LOVE IS A QUESTION.

LOVE IS THE ANSWER.

Love is a dark pit.

LOVE IS A SWEET TORMENT.

He loves me....He loves me not....
He loves me... He loves me not...

Love is not something you find,
but something that finds you.

Love is not what you say, but what you do.

Love is like playing checkers. You have to know which man to move.

LOVE IS DEAD.

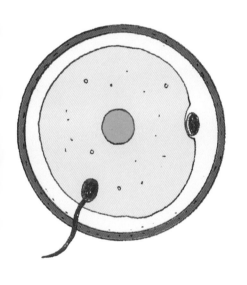

LOVE IS ALIVE.

LOVE IS PATIENT.

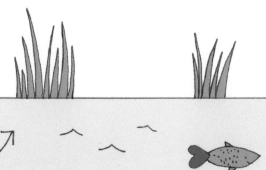

LOVE IS A CHOICE.

LOVE IS NOT A CHOICE.

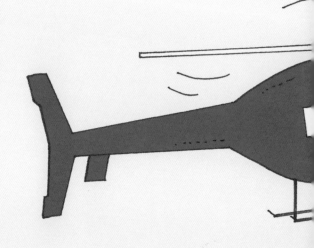

Love is letting go of fear.

LOVE IS A GAME.

Love is love.

LOVE IS SOMETHING
SENT FROM HEAVEN
TO WORRY THE HELL
OUT OF YOU.

LOVE IS OVERRATED.

Love is a great beautifier.

LOVE IS BLIND.

Love is a flower.

Love is a verb.

LOVE IS A BOURGEOIS CONSTRUCT.

LOVE IS ALL

YOU NEED.

ATTRIBUTIONS

• •

"Love is much nicer to be in than an automobile accident, a tight girdle, a higher tax bracket, or a holding pattern over Philadelphia." —JUDITH VIORST

"Love is a battlefield." —PAT BENATAR

"Love is like a red, red rose." —ROBERT BURNS

"Love is not the dying moan of a distant violin— it's the twang of a bedspring." —S. J. PERELMAN

"Love is old, love is new / love is all, love is you." —THE BEATLES

"Love is singing karaoke 'Under Pressure' and letting the other person sing the Freddie Mercury part." —MINDY KALING

"Love is the delightful interval between meeting a beautiful girl and discovering she looks like a haddock." —JOHN BARRYMORE

"Love is like oxygen / You get too much you get too high / Not enough and you're gonna die." —SWEET

"Love is a burning thing." —JOHNNY CASH

"Love is metaphysical gravity." —BUCKMINSTER FULLER

"Love is the drug I'm thinking of." —ROXY MUSIC

"Love is like playing checkers. You have to know which man to move." —JACKIE 'MOMS' MABLEY

"Love is something sent from Heaven to worry the Hell out of you." —DOLLY PARTON

"Love is a great beautifier." —LOUISA MAY ALCOTT

"Love is a verb." —CLARE BOOTH LUCE

"Love is a bourgeois construct." —PET SHOP BOYS

"Love is all you need." —THE BEATLES

LOVE IS A METAPHOR.